How to Be

Happy

No Matter What!

Edited by
Sarah Nagel

Blue Mountain Press™
Boulder, Colorado

We gratefully acknowledge the permission granted by the following authors, publishers, and authors' representatives to reprint poems or excerpts from their publications: Susan Polis Schutz for "Find Happiness in Everything You Do" and "The world was made to be beautiful...." Copyright © 1983, 1993 by Stephen Schutz and Susan Polis Schutz. All rights reserved. PrimaDonna Entertainment Corp. for "Don't Let Anything Steal Your Joy," "Choose to Be Happy," and "Start the day believing..." by Donna Fargo. Copyright © 2005, 2010, 2011 by PrimaDonna Entertainment Corp. All rights reserved. Hay House, Inc., Carlsbad, CA, for "Happiness will always bring out..." and "Your intention to love..." from HAPPINESS NOW! TIMELESS WISDOM FOR FEELING GOOD FAST by Robert Holden, PhD. Copyright © 1998 by Robert Holden. Revised copyright © 2007. All rights reserved. Dutton Signet, a division of Penguin Group (USA), Inc., for "You already know the key to..." and "It is not up to your boss..." from LIVING WELL EMOTIONALLY by Montel Williams. Copyright © 2009 by Mountain Movers, Inc. All rights reserved. Broadway Books, a division of Random House, Inc., for "Above all, remember to be..." by Gerry Laybourne, "Don't be so worried about what..." by Trisha Yearwood, and "You're going to have to learn..." by Picabo Street from WHAT I KNOW NOW: LETTERS TO MY YOUNGER SELF by Ellyn Spragins. Copyright © 2006 by Ellyn Spragins. All rights reserved. And for "This approach of focusing on the positive..." from THE HAPPINESS MAKEOVER by M. J. Ryan. Copyright © 2005 by M. J. Ryan. All rights reserved.

Acknowledgments are continued on the last page.

Library of Congress Control Number: 2011907496
ISBN: 978-1-59842-624-3

Blue Mountain Arts, Inc.
P.O. Box 4549, Boulder, Colorado 80306

Contents

(Authors listed in order of first appearance)

Choose to Be Happy

You've got this moment... You can choose to be happy or unhappy. You can choose what you think, what you say, and how you feel. You can choose to be hopeful or hopeless, to respond angrily or cheerfully, to be bored or interested.

You've got this day... No matter what the weather is like, you can choose what kind of day it will be — beautiful or awful or somewhere in between. You can choose what you will do and what you won't — to give up or give in or go on. You have a choice to do something or nothing, to start now or later. You can choose your attitude about what you're facing.

You've got your life... If you're not happy, satisfied, encouraged, and hopeful, you're cheating yourself. You can talk and talk to yourself about what you need to do to honor your life, but if you don't turn those thoughts into actions, you're just playing games and giving up to whatever comes to mind.

You've got the power to make choices... Your life is the manifestation of the choices you make each moment and each day. When you use this awesome gift to your best advantage, you can be happy no matter what.

✳ Donna Fargo

Let Your Spirit Shine

*H*appiness will always bring out the best in you. You were born to be happy. Happiness is natural. It suits you completely. You look good and you feel good when you let happiness ooze from within you. Your step is light, your mind is free, and your spirit soars when you let happiness *happen*. The whole world responds well to you.

When you're truly happy, you're radiant and you function fully. Above all, you are loving, for the essence of happiness is love. You're also naturally kind, generous, open, warm, and friendly. This is because where there's true happiness, there is no fear, no doubt, and no anxiety. You're unrestrained and uninhibited. You are fully present, here and now, and not lost in some past or future.

When you're truly happy, you're on point and on purpose. You're also very real. It is, after all, impossible to be happy and play small, to be happy and hide, to be happy and inauthentic, to be happy and defensive....

True happiness is also very attractive in that it literally attracts great things. Happiness, by its very nature, encourages trust, spontaneity, optimism, and enthusiasm — all of which bring great gifts. In particular, when you dare to be happy, you find that people instinctively gravitate to you and like you, although they may not know why. Maybe it's something to do with your smile. Whatever it is, your happiness is an inspiration and a gift to everyone. *Everyone benefits from true happiness... everyone benefits from your happiness.*

✳ Robert Holden, PhD

Embrace Optimism

You already know the key to happiness. Your momma told you, your grandmother told you, you know it. Stop the garbage thoughts and think positive. You have to make the conscious decision. When you get up and look in the mirror, don't say, "Oh, I hate my hair. I can't believe it's so curly." Instead, say, "Dang, I've got myself some beautiful hair. I might want to cut it, but it's beautiful. Ain't nobody gonna take that from me, 'cause it's mine!"

✳ Montel Williams

Above all, remember to be your own best friend. Turn off the radio station in your head that points out your failures.

✳ Gerry Laybourne

Somehow telling people to "count their blessings" tends to get them angry, as though that phrase, though trite by now, had no merit or wisdom. What makes it so difficult for you to accept what is light, when the darkness is so oppressive? One would think that you'd enthusiastically jump toward the light! The answer is simple, really — you don't want there to be darkness; you want to conquer, punish, or eliminate the darkness. Generally, none of that is possible.

Searching for the light is a better way. Switch from cursing the darkness to celebrating the light.

※ Dr. Laura Schlessinger

*A*lways think on the bright side —
no matter what life brings
to your day.
You'll gain a treasure within your soul
that no worry or hardship
can ever take away.

＊ Isaac Purcell

*T*hink about the good things in life,
like sunshine, holidays, feeling loved,
special friendships, and laughter. Think
about rainbows, butterflies, and beautiful
sunsets, and feel loved, cared about, and
accepted. Remember that in life, although
there is some bad stuff, good things
really do happen, too. And then smile.

＊ Maria Mullins

*H*ave hope. Because it works wonders for those who have it. Be optimistic. Because people who expect things to turn out for the best often set the stage to receive a beautiful result.

Put things in perspective. Because some things are important, and others are definitely not.

Remember that beyond the clouds, the sun is still shining. Meet each challenge and give it all you've got.

Count your blessings. Be inspired to climb your ladders and have some nice, long talks with your wishing stars. Be strong and patient. Be gentle and wise.

Believe in happy endings. Because you are the author of the story of your life.

✳ Douglas Pagels

Savor the Present Moment

What I learned was that my enjoyment of life has everything to do with being "in the moment" and that the only thing that keeps me (or anyone) from being fully in the moment is our misunderstanding of the nature of our own thinking — how it pulls us away from the moment, confuses us, and stresses us. I realized that everything I ever needed is right here, right now — as long as my thinking doesn't carry me away from this moment. I learned that there is nothing in the future to rush off to that can offer me anything more than *this* precious moment that you and I are in every instant.

✳ Joseph Bailey

$\mathcal{B}$y being in the present moment,
you will be able to let go of past
regrets and future worries by focusing
on the here and now. Living in a state
of contentment means that you don't
lose sight of the big picture, but that
you allow yourself to revel in where
you are at this moment.

※ Kimberly Wilson

$\mathcal{J}$ust focus on "right now" —
not the future or the past...
just this one moment
right here where you stand.

※ Ashley Rice

Free Yourself from Worry

One of the quickest ways to disturb peace of mind is to worry about the future. I call this falling in the future hole. Future hole self-talk statements often begin with: "What if...," "I couldn't handle it if...," "I'm afraid that...." It's times like these when we need to remember the biblical observation: "Sufficient unto the day is the trouble therein." We can handle what comes our way today, but if we add what might happen tomorrow or two years from now we are seriously jeopardizing our peace of mind....

If we find ourselves worrying about the future, we need to pull our mind back to today, telling ourselves, "I can handle today, right now, this minute. Tomorrow is not here. Now is all I need to be concerned with."

* Sue Patton Thoele

*M*ost worries are future-based. They revolve around things that, in most cases, will *never* happen. Concentrate on the present and the future will take care of itself.

✳ Paul Wilson

*D*on't be so worried about what everybody else thinks of you, and don't think your happiness depends on someone else. I want you to just trust yourself. Trust that if you take care of yourself on the inside, follow your instincts, and let yourself evolve naturally, your potential for happiness will be so much greater.

✳ Trisha Yearwood

Remember What Is Most Important

It's not having everything go right;
it's facing whatever goes wrong.
It's not being without fear;
it's having the determination
   to go on in spite of it.

What is most important is not
   where you stand,
but the direction you're going in.
It's more than never having bad moments;
it's knowing you are always
   bigger than the moment.
It's believing you have already
   been given everything
you need to handle life.
It's not being able to rid
   the world of all its injustices;
it's being able to rise above them.
It's the belief in your heart
   that there will always be
more good than bad in the world.

Remember to live just this one day
and not add tomorrow's troubles
    to today's load.
Remember that every day ends
and brings a new tomorrow
full of exciting new things.
Love what you do,
    do the best you can,
and always remember
    how much you are loved.

                       ✳ Vickie M. Worsham

Celebrate Your Uniqueness

You are something — and someone — very special. You really are. No one else in this entire world is exactly like you, and there are so many beautiful things about you. You're a one-of-a-kind treasure, uniquely here in this space and time. You are here to shine in your own wonderful way, sharing your smile in the best way you can, and remembering all the while that a little light somewhere makes a brighter light everywhere. You can — and you do — make a wonderful contribution to this world.

✳ Douglas Pagels

Do your very best to understand what you've *got*: the wonderful power of your own heart, soul, and hands... which is much, much more than a lot.

✳ Ashley Rice

Be Your Own Best Friend

You're going to have to learn how to pat yourself on the back eventually. Start now. It's not gloating. It's taking pleasure in life's goodness.

* Picabo Street

We're quick to recognize and support others in their achievements, but we put the words "I'm just" in front of our job title or role in life, as if it's not even worthy of a mention. We need to do better for ourselves.... Whether it's a promotion or something as small as learning a new computer skill or getting through a checklist of errands, we have to learn to say to ourselves, "Good job! I'm proud of you!"

* Queen Latifah

Believe in Yourself

Every goal that has ever been reached
began with just one step —
and the belief that
it could be attained.

Dreams really can come true,
but they are most often the result
of hard work, determination,
    and persistence.

When the end of the journey
seems impossible to reach,
remember that all you need to do
is take one more step.

Stay focused on your goal
and remember...
each small step will bring you
    a little closer.

When the road becomes
    hard to travel
and it feels as if you'll never
    reach the end...
look deep inside your heart
and you will find strength
    you never knew you had.

* Jason Blume

Trust your decisions and feelings
and do what is best for you.
The future will work itself out;
you're the kind of person
who can make it happen.
Don't let anyone else's negativity
influence your dreams, values, or hopes.
Focus on what you can change
and let go of what you can't.
You know your own worth,
what you've accomplished,
and what you're capable of.
Step boldly and confidently
    into your future
where happiness, success,
and dreams await you.

You have the potential
    for greatness...
never give up.

※ Barbara Cage

$\mathcal{K}$eep looking forward to the future... to all you might be. Don't let old mistakes or misfortunes hold you down: learn from them, forgive yourself — or others — and move on. Do not be bothered or discouraged by adversity. Instead, meet it as a challenge. Be empowered by the courage it takes you to overcome obstacles. Learn something new every day. Be interested in others and what they might teach you, but do not look for yourself in other people's approval. As far as who you are and who you will become goes... the answer is always within yourself. Believe in yourself. Follow your heart and your dreams. You, like everyone, will make mistakes. But so long as you are true to the strength within your own heart... you can never go wrong.

✳ Ashley Rice

Hold On to Hope

We all have days when we wonder how we can keep pressing forward — when things don't really come together as we had hoped and we feel discouraged and dejected. It happens to everyone.

On days like these, it's essential to remember that life is constantly in motion and things simply can't stay the way they are right now. Hope still exists in ways big and small, trust will find its way back to you, and a little faith can create a lot of change. Above all other things, remember you are loved.

Take these thoughts into your heart, and let them fill you up. Then take a deep breath, and begin again.

* Elizabeth Rose

$\mathcal{L}$ife has a way of throwing us off course,
surprising us into making changes
we weren't planning on making.
Things may get difficult,
and we may struggle to do what's right.
But each new day brings new hope
and offers us a new chance to get it right.

Don't focus on what was.
Look forward to what can be,
and then do all you can to make it a reality.
Life is what you make of it,
and the challenges that come your way
are opportunities to right what is wrong.
Don't get discouraged, and don't give up.
You have it all inside yourself,
and you can overcome anything
if you put your mind to it.

✳ Paula Michele Adams

Try an Instant Pick-Me-Up

1. **Seek out the positive.** Even if you cannot see a silver lining at the moment, start to look for it.

2. **Appreciate the beauty of nature.** Spend time outdoors, and you will feel more peaceful and connected with life.

3. **Write a letter to a friend.** Each time you reach out to another person, you experience the very basic human joy of sharing yourself.

4. **Step out of hopelessness.** Take a realistic look at your self-doubts, and find something to value in your life.

5. **Do something physical.** Exercise is sometimes all you need to shift negative energy into something purposeful and more engaging.

6. **Use bright and positive language.** Lift your tone and your vocabulary, and you will immediately feel better.

7. **Remind yourself that everything changes.** Optimists stay mindful of this fact, especially when times are hard.

8. **Enjoy something.** Watch a favorite movie, phone your best friend... and watch those blues disappear.

9. **Encourage someone else.** As soon as you tap into the encouraging habit, you will miraculously find yourself feeling encouraged, too.

10. **Look at the bigger picture.** View the situation from a wider perspective. If you need to act, then do; if not, just let it go.

※ Lynda Field

Don't Let Anything Steal Your Joy

Choose to be well in every way. Choose to be happy no matter what. Decide that each day will be good just because you're alive. You have power over your thoughts and feelings. Don't let your circumstances dictate how you feel. Don't let your thoughts and feelings color your situation blue or desperate.

Even if you don't have everything you want, even if you're in pain or in need, you can choose to be joyful no matter what you're experiencing. You are more than your body, your physical presence, and your material possessions. You are spirit. You have your mind, heart, and soul, and there is always something to be thankful for.

Decide that life is good and you are special. Decide to enjoy today. Decide that you will live life to the fullest now, no matter what. Trust that you will change what needs changing, but also decide that you're not going to put off enjoying life just because you don't have everything you want now. Steadfastly refuse to let anything steal your joy. Choose to be happy... and you will be!

✳ Donna Fargo

Keep Things in Perspective

Never forget what a treasure you are ✳ Try to realize how important you are in the eyes of the world ✳ No matter where you go, hopes and hearts travel beside you every step of the way ✳ Even though difficulties come to everyone, it isn't fair when they hang around longer than they should ✳ But until a new day comes along, trust that you'll always be strong enough to see things through ✳ Remember how much strength and courage you have inside ✳

You can find all the patience it takes ✳
You can turn to the times in the past
when challenges were met, when you
survived, when you were rewarded
with success, and when you learned to
believe in so much within you ✳ You
have so much going for you, and you're
going to see your way through anything
that comes along ✳ Brighter days are
going to find a way to shine in your
windows and chase away any blues ✳
Because no one deserves more smiles,
success, friendship, or love ...than you ✳

✳ Brian Gill

Trust That Everything Will Fall into Place

Life is like a giant puzzle.
Each of us has a picture in our minds
    of how our lives will turn out.
We keep adding pieces, one at a time,
attempting to create that beautiful picture.
If one piece does not fit, we replace it
    with another.
We never get all the pieces in the right place
    on the first try.
It's all about experimenting until each piece
    fits together with the next.
Though our futures may not be clear
    or turn out exactly as we expected,
each of us has the strength inside to put
    the puzzle together.
We just have to look for the right pieces.
It may seem impossible, but keep striving.
Life's pieces have a way of falling into place
    when you least expect it.

✳ Renée M. Brtalik

Give Your Dreams
a Chance

Remember that transformation
is not only possible,
but it happens every day —
think of butterflies, seeds,
and springtime.

Our world is full of new beginnings.
It is larger than any of us can comprehend.
Take heart, believe in big skies
and wide-open spaces,
and hold on to the promise
of mysteries and magic.
There is space for your dreams to grow.
The future may astonish you.

* Rebecca Brown

Never Forget Who You Are

Don't ever lose sight of the gift that is you. Remember what you're made of. Remember what's flowing in your veins. Remember what you were given, and remember what you went out and created on your own. Like any great masterpiece, you're not done yet. Inside you is the best of everyone who has come before you — and the best of everyone yet to be. You can forget some of what life hands you, but never, ever forget who you are... You are a gift to the world!

* Rachel Snyder

Remember the depth and core of you;
    remember the strength and light of you.
Remember the love of you.
Remember where you came from
    and where you've been.
Remember that nothing can destroy you.
Life can only make you bigger, better,
    and brighter, if you allow it to do so.
Remember to always
    help light the way for others.
Think of it not as your work
    or even your purpose,
        but as your destiny.
You are empowering and brilliant
    beyond comprehension.
You are creative and inspiring.
Remember this always,
    as you continue being you.

                            ✳ Jane Almarie Lewis

Open Your Heart to Love

There is only one happiness in life,
to love and be loved.

✳ George Sand

Your intention to love, no matter
what, is the absolute key to happiness.
Think about it. Try, if you can, to hate
someone and be happy. Try to resent
somebody and be joyous. Try to be
angry at someone and be peaceful.
Try to judge someone and feel free.
Try to control someone and not feel
controlled. Try to be fully independent
and intimate. Try to cheat somebody
and feel safe. It can't happen, because
what you do to another you're doing
to yourself....

Put love first — above everything.

✳ Robert Holden, PhD

You need close long-term relationships,
you need to be able to confide in others,
you need to belong. Studies show that if
you have five or more friends with whom to
discuss an important matter, you're far more
likely to describe yourself as "very happy."...

No matter what they're doing, people tend to
feel happier when they're with other people.
One study showed that whether you are
exercising, commuting, or doing housework,
everything is more fun in company. This
is true not just of extroverts but, perhaps
surprisingly, of introverts as well.

✳ Gretchen Rubin

Love often starts in little ways.
It comes quietly with a smile,
a glance, or a touch,
but you know it's there
because suddenly you're not alone
and the sadness inside you is gone.

✳ Vickie M. Worsham

Practice Gratitude

Gratitude is the finest prayer our souls can utter. Gratitude is also an attitude. As with any attitude, it can be nurtured, cultivated, and changed if need be. Gratitude, like laughter and humor, lifts our spirits and hearts and encourages us to ascend into realms of joy and appreciation. It makes us thankful for the incredible gift of life that we've been given and for the people who have chosen to share it with us.

Gratitude gentles even the roughest roads and gives wings to the heart. Buoyed by gratitude, we can sail over most situations while keeping a healthy, and even joyful, perspective on the landscape of our lives. Gratitude is communion with God and graces our relationships with a high and holy soul-connection. Gratitude is meditation in action. Gratitude is the single most powerful medicine for physical, mental, and spiritual health for us individually, and for our planet as a whole.

* Sue Patton Thoele

*I*n those moments when I have found myself gasping for air, feeling that I was going under, I've discovered that *gratitude truly is my life preserver.* Even in the most turbulent waters, choosing gratitude rescues me from myself and my runaway emotions. It buoys me on the grace of God and keeps me from drowning in what otherwise would be my natural bent toward doubt, negativity, discouragement, and anxiety.

* Nancy Leigh DeMoss

*B*e content with what you have; rejoice in the way things are. When you realize there is nothing lacking, the whole world belongs to you.

* Lao Tzu

*G*ratitude is heaven itself.

* William Blake

Appreciate the Simple Things

The world was made
to be beautiful —
but sometimes we get caught up in
everyday actions
completely forgetting about this
completely forgetting that what
is truly important
are the simple, basic things in life —
honest, pure emotions
surrounded by the majestic beauty of nature
We need to concentrate on
the freeness and peacefulness of nature
and not on the driven material aspects of life
We need to smell the clear air
after the rainfall
and appreciate the good in things
We need to remember that
we are here for a short time
and that every day should count for something and
that every day we should be thankful
for all the natural beauty
The world is a wonderful place
and we are so lucky to be a part of it

＊ Susan Polis Schutz

$\mathcal{E}$njoying life does not mean we have something exciting going on all the time; it simply means we need to learn to enjoy simple, everyday things. Most of life is rather ordinary, but we are supernaturally equipped with the power of God to live ordinary everyday life in an extraordinary way.

✳ Joyce Meyer

$\mathcal{T}$he nicest and sweetest days are not those on which anything very splendid or wonderful or exciting happens but just those that bring simple little pleasures, following one another softly, like pearls slipping off a string.

✳ L. M. Montgomery

$\mathcal{B}$e glad every morning that you've been given a brand-new opportunity to fulfill your hopes and dreams.

Be glad for all the seasons and the beauty they bring to your life: the hopeful springs, the blossoming summers, the brilliant autumns, and the quiet fire of winter days.

Be glad for your talents, whatever they may be; they make you absolutely unique, and they were given so that you could make your own special contribution to this earth.

✳ Jon Peyton

$\mathcal{T}$o me every hour of the light and dark is a miracle, Every cubic inch of space is a miracle.

✳ Walt Whitman

*H*onor the beauty that crosses your path each and every day, such as flowering, scented trees and bushes, a fallow daffodil pushing up from the barren earth, artwork in the office, or colorful fruit displays at the grocery store. Acknowledge what you accomplish daily, even if it's simply getting out of bed or getting to the office on time in clean clothes. Otherwise, our mindfulness is stuck on moving toward the future, rather than being in the present and encouraging ourselves along the way.

✳ Kimberly Wilson

*W*hy not learn to enjoy the little things — there are so many of them.

✳ Anonymous

Slow Down and Relax

*L*ife can be so busy, and we sometimes take for granted the important little things that make us smile. Look at the sunset, share a cup of coffee with your best friend, or hear the wind rustle through the trees. Take some time to listen to life, feel the sun on your face, and stop to watch butterflies in your garden.

* Carol Schelling

I've heard it said that every day you need half an hour of quiet time for yourself... unless you're incredibly busy and stressed, in which case you need an hour. I promise you, it is there. Fight tooth and nail to find time, to make it. It is our true wealth, this moment, this hour, this day.

* Anne Lamott

Cars often have a helpful red light that blinks, alerting us to low fuel. And when we truly listen to ourselves, we can also hear the message, "Help! I'm running out of gas." We may hear the message, and yet ignore it.

Being a good friend to ourselves means hearing and heeding the empty-tank message. We all need rest and relaxation, and we all deserve to rest and relax. In order to feel loving and be able to snap and crackle with energy, we need to give ourselves permission to snap, crackle, then plop....

We need to allow ourselves some time each day to rest and relax in our own unique way. Only we know when it is time to fill up our tank.

＊ Sue Patton Thoele

Revel in the Beauty of Nature

There is truly something magical to be found within nature. Take a bike ride through your local park. Pack your lunch and head to a city park to dine mid-workday. Go camping — yes, car camping counts. Enjoy a Sunday afternoon hike or stroll through your nearby state park. Take a fall foliage tour through the Northeast. Rent a cabin in the country as often as you can. Snowshoe by moonlight. Nap under a big oak tree. Go rock climbing. Splash around at the beach.... Nature has a calming effect that can help keep us, and our trite everyday dramas, in perspective.

✳ Kimberly Wilson

Climb the mountains and get their good tidings. Nature's peace will flow into you as sunshine flows into trees. The winds will blow their own freshness into you... while cares will drip off like autumn leaves.

✳ John Muir

There is good in life every day. Take a few minutes to distract yourself from your concerns — long enough to draw strength from a tree or to find pleasure in a bird's song.

✳ Pamela Owens Renfro

Cherish Each Moment

You've got to celebrate... life isn't promised, and those special moments need to be cherished for whatever they are, whether they're a graduation, a promotion, a wedding day, or even a small thing like losing five pounds. We get so caught up in our business that too often we forget how to live, and we miss all those moments that should be giving us joy.

✳ Queen Latifah

Life is not measured by the number
of breaths we take,
but by the moments that take
our breath away.

✳ Anonymous

*E*very morning, wake with the awe
   of just being alive.
Each day, discover the magnificent,
   awesome beauty in the world.
Explore and embrace life in yourself
   and in everything you see.
Live every day well.
Let a little sunshine out as well as in.
Create your own rainbows.
Be open to possibilities.
Believe in miracles!

                       ✷ Vickie M. Worsham

*N*othing is worth more than this day.
                 ✷ Johann Wolfgang von Goethe

*J*oy is being in love and sleeping in the sunshine and running down a mountain path with the swiftness of a deer in the springtime. Joy expands your heart and opens your soul. Joy is snowflakes and slipping on the ice and getting up so you can slip all over again and never even feeling the cold. Living in joy doesn't mean putting on a happy face. It means that joy is at the core of who you are and always have been. Joy is strong enough to carry you through the darkness and the pain into a place where joy still resides in ultimate measure. Seek to find joy and let joy fill your life.

✳ Rachel Snyder

Ten Ways to Find Joy

✳ Stay positive! (Hopeful people are happier people.) ✳ Choose wisely. (Good choices will come back to bless you.) ✳ Remember what matters. (The present moment. The good people in it. Hopes and dreams and feelings.) ✳ Don't stress out over things you can't control. (Just don't.) ✳ Count every blessing. (Even the little ones add up to a lot.) ✳ Be good to your body. (It's the only one you get.) ✳ And listen to the wishes of your heart. (It always seems to know what's true, what's right, what to do, and where to go with your life.) ✳ Understand how special you are. ✳ Realize how strong you can be. ✳ And know that YES, you're going to make it through, no matter what.

✳ Douglas Pagels

Find Happiness
in Everything You Do

Find happiness in nature
in the beauty of a mountain
in the serenity of the sea
Find happiness in friendship
in the fun of doing things together
in the sharing and understanding
Find happiness in your family
in the stability of knowing
    that someone cares
in the strength of love and honesty
Find happiness in yourself
in your mind and body
in your values and achievements
Find happiness in
everything
you
do

    ✳ Susan Polis Schutz

Start each day believing that life is good and it's good for you. Believe that opportunities are on the way. Believe that you've got what it takes to do whatever you want to do. Lose the fears and regrets. Lighten up, and laugh out loud.

Don't be afraid to get a little wild. You were born to be free, so celebrate yourself in style. Let your mind ramble, and just follow your heart. Be thankful and let go of anything that brings you down. Be happy and have fun every day.

✳ Donna Fargo

Laugh as much as possible. Let in the good times and get through the bad. Be happy with who and where you are. You are in the right place, and your heart is leading you on the way to a great tomorrow.

✳ Ashley Rice

Give Yourself the Gift of Happiness

This approach of focusing on the positive is not a plea to ignore or deny the challenges, sorrows, and grief in our lives. They are real. And it doesn't mean that we feel fabulous all the livelong day. But the possibility of experiencing the joy of being alive, of appreciating what we can in our circumstances, of letting go of unnecessary burdens, of giving to others — is also real. We have what we need to be happy. In every moment, we can choose where to focus our attention and therefore how we feel. The difficulties of our lives get a lot of our mental air time and sap a great deal of our life force. How about giving equal time to happiness?

✳ M. J. Ryan

*I*t is not up to your boss to make you happy.

It is not your friend's job or your preacher's job and it's not up to your doctor or psychiatrist.

It is not even your family's job to make you happy.

It is all up to you! Life is what you deem it.

It's important to understand that happiness is something you do, not something you find....

You create your own life. You create your own happiness. You make the choice whether you are happy or unhappy. It's not the circumstances that force the happiness or unhappiness on you.

＊ Montel Williams

*B*y an act of your will, choose to start enjoying your life right now. Learn to enjoy your family, your friends, your health, your work; enjoy everything in your life. Happiness is a decision you make, not an emotion you feel. Certainly there are times in all our lives when bad things happen, or things don't turn out as we had hoped. But that's when we must make a decision that we're going to be happy in spite of our circumstances.

＊ Joel Osteen

Acknowledgments continued...

We gratefully acknowledge the permission granted by the following authors, publishers, and authors' representatives to reprint poems or excerpts from their publications: HarperCollins Publishers for "Somehow telling people to..." from STOP WHINING, START LIVING by Dr. Laura Schlessinger. Copyright © 2008 by Dr. Laura Schlessinger. All rights reserved. And for "What I learned was that..." by Joseph Bailey from SLOWING DOWN TO THE SPEED OF LIFE by Richard Carlson and Joseph Bailey. Copyright © 1997 by Richard Carlson and Joseph Bailey. All rights reserved. And for "You need close long-term relationships..." from THE HAPPINESS PROJECT by Gretchen Rubin. Copyright © 2009 by Gretchen Rubin. All rights reserved. New World Library, Novato, CA, www.newworldlibrary.com, for "By being in the present moment..." from HIP TRANQUIL CHICK by Kimberly Wilson. Copyright © 2006 by Kimberly Wilson. All rights reserved. And for "Honor the beauty that crosses..." and "There is truly something magical to be found..." from TRANQUILISTA: MASTERING THE ART OF ENLIGHTENED WORK AND MINDFUL PLAY by Kimberly Wilson. Copyright © 2010 by Kimberly Wilson. All rights reserved. Red Wheel/Weiser, LLC, www.redwheelweiser.com, for "One of the quickest ways...," "Gratitude is the finest prayer...," and "Cars often have a helpful red light..." from THE WOMAN'S BOOK OF SOUL by Sue Patton Thoele. Copyright © 1998 by Sue Patton Thoele. All rights reserved. Dutton, a division of Penguin Group (USA), Inc., for "Most worries are future-based..." from THE LITTLE BOOK OF CALM by Paul Wilson. Copyright © 1996 by Paul Wilson. All rights reserved. Grand Central Publishing for "We're quick to recognize..." and "You've got to celebrate..." from PUT ON YOUR CROWN by Queen Latifah. Copyright © 2010 by Queen Latifah, Inc. Reprinted by permission of Grand Central Publishing. All rights reserved. Jason Blume for "Believe in Yourself." Copyright © 2005 by Jason Blume. All rights reserved. Paula Michele Adams for "Life has a way of throwing us off course...." Copyright © 2011 by Paula Michele Adams. All rights reserved. Lynda Field for "Try an Instant Pick-Me-Up." Copyright © 2011 by Lynda Field. All rights reserved. Rachel Snyder for "Don't ever lose sight of the gift..." and "Joy is being in love...." Copyright © 2008, 2011 by Rachel Snyder. All rights reserved. Jane Almarie Lewis for "Remember the depth and core of you...." Copyright © 2011 by Jane Almarie Lewis. All rights reserved. Moody Publishers for "In those moments when..." from CHOOSING GRATITUDE by Nancy Leigh DeMoss. Copyright © 2009 by Nancy Leigh DeMoss. All rights reserved. Warner Faith for "Enjoying life does not mean..." from SEVEN THINGS THAT STEAL YOUR JOY by Joyce Meyer. Copyright © 2004 by Joyce Meyer. Reprinted by permission of Warner Faith. All rights reserved. And for "By an act of your will..." from YOUR BEST LIFE NOW by Joel Osteen. Copyright © 2005 by Joel Osteen Publishing. Reprinted by permission of Warner Faith. All rights reserved. Anne Lamott and The Wylie Agency LLC for "I've heard it said that..." from "Time Lost and Found" by Anne Lamott (*Sunset*: April 2010). Copyright © 2010 by Anne Lamott. Reprinted by permission. All rights reserved.

A careful effort has been made to trace the ownership of selections used in this anthology in order to obtain permission to reprint copyrighted material and give proper credit to the copyright owners. If any error or omission has occurred, it is completely inadvertent, and we would like to make corrections in future editions provided that written notification is made to the publisher:

BLUE MOUNTAIN ARTS, INC., P.O. Box 4549, Boulder, Colorado 80306.